choice

choice

an anthology of irish poetry
selected by the poets themselves
with a comment on their choice

Desmond Egan (signature)

edited by desmond egan
and michael hartnett

(1.4.96 Queens College) (handwritten)

*Published by The Goldsmith Press The Curragh Ireland
and printed by Leinster Leader Ltd.*

*First edition 1973
Second edition 1979*

Contents

Introduction

Making an anthology is the most thankless of all literary tasks. In the eyes of editors, poets and critics, all anthologies seem to be full of unnecessary inclusions and inexplicable omissions. And yet the idea of having a widely representative collection of verse by contemporary Irish poets seemed worthwhile. In each case, the choice of poem has been left to the poet, who adds a commentary.

All the poems here then, are by living Irish poets. Many are well known, some not so well known. The poems are not necessarily the poets' best, but are those which the poets *like* best: it is hardly possible that any poet still writing believes his best poem is behind him. In general we looked for shorter poems but anyone who felt he would be better represented by a longer poem was not denied his choice. And since that choice lay with the authors, this anthology, for once, is not a critical one in the usual sense. Nevertheless, a certain standard had to be maintained. Whether the poems we ourselves choose are up to that standard, we leave to the reader to decide; each is included in an Appendix.

We hope that anyone reading the collection will get an accurate enough idea of what is going on in Irish poetry at the moment. That is the aim of the anthology.

Desmond Egan
Michael Hartnett, 1973.

choice

Leland Bardwell

This is a narrative poem describing the reaction of the public on the morning of the execution of Ruth Ellis in 1954. I choose it because I think it expresses the futility of this aspect of the British Legal system as well as the futility of her crime.

The fact that the subsequent outcry to the hanging of Ruth Ellis among others, caused the repeal of the laws regarding Capital punishment is alluded to by the irony of the last three lines; she was neither martyr nor saint but she was the last woman to be hanged in Britain and thereby an important pivotal point in the evolution of British justice although the passage of time has obliterated neither the outrage of hanging nor her personal tragedy.

The central stanza about the breakfast is, of course, not direct reportage but a symbolic representation of the guilt of the three parties mentioned and for which only one was about to be punished by legalised murder.

For Ruth Ellis

In Camden Road, London, N.7
And that was long before
marching became the norm
A brisk watery sun
rose surly on a bank of trees
As hysteria mounted,
took over the precinct
like a burning house
in the mess of dogs
and bulging rubber faces
bursting into the clamour

with their clear morning faces
like soap bubbles in the sun
crying REPRIEVE
and half of them did not know
the meaning of the word.

In the breakfast of their equal loss
the Queen
the Home Secretary
and Ruth Ellis
had eaten well

That was the only news
SENSATIONAL

Please Mr. Pierrepoint
another lover died outside a Hampstead pub
who took the trade of dalliance and sport
But eternity plays in a jealous mart
we kill for stupidity, not for love
from hopelessness to helplessness
from dearth to dearth returned

But behind the useless bulging of that oaken door
somewhere undefeated the hangman stands,
immutable as a snow-man
If her rope is a makeshift cross
what good comes out of a tragedy that's pure
or a comedy that's harsh?

Samuel Beckett

The following poem is the author's own translation from the French. Characteristically, Mr. Beckett made no comment.

my way is in the sand flowing
between the shingle and the dune
the summer rain rains on my life
on me my life harrying fleeing
to its beginning to its end

my peace is there in the receding mist
when I may cease from treading these
                              long shifting thresholds
and live the space of a door
that opens and shuts

Eavan Boland

The rationalization of a lyric resembles the theory of love: it may emerge afterwards; it can never precede a poem, and should not restrict it.

That said, I think I may annotate this poem with the remark that it is taken from the reported conflict of Athene, goddess of war in Athenian myth. According to that story, her attraction to war was once cast into doubt, when she found a pipe in a wood and playing it, discovered a simpler power, more elusive and no less real, than any she exercised in her unquestioned role as mascot of belligerence.

Athene's song

From my father's head I sprung
Goddess of the war, created
Partisan and soldier's physic,
My symbols boast and brazen gong
Until I found in Athens' wood
Upon my knees a new music.

When I played my pipe of bone,
Robbed and whittled from a stag
Every bird became a lover,
Every lover to its tone
Learned the truth of song and brag:
Fish sprung in the full river.

Peace became the toy of power
When other noises broke my sleep,
Like dreams I saw the hot ranks
And heroes in another flower
Than any there. I broke my pipe
Remembering their shouts, their thanks:

Beside the water, lost and mute
Lies my pipe and like my mind
Remains unknown, remains unknown
And in some hollow taking part
With my heart against my hand
Holds its peace and holds its own.

Francis Boylan

I have no favourite *poem—at least not yet. I choose this one simply because it is under the twenty line limit. Any poem I write I try to see as part of something which may be entire. However, in so far as I publish a poem at all, I hope that it manifests in some way the absolute truth of this statement:* The reality of things themselves is their light.

Paul Cezanne

Winter is here once more,
Once more I stand on frozen ground
Looking at the picture.
I move an inch and thus I grow
Because the mind grows bound
In the intensity of a thrush's gesture.
The floors of sequins change
And every inch brings something new and strange.

That is enough my life,
To live that tension like the thrush —
Paul Cezanne, for weeks
Held in the one angle of his eye
Till hand and eye and brush
Moved in his vision like a breeze.
The floors of sequins change
And every inch brings something new and strange.

Juanita Casey

As a female I've always been expected to Do Something About the Dust. And never have which is possibly why three husbands rapidly left in a Cloud Of. And why I, now living in the manner of the Zen Masters who happily beat each other over the head shouting Old Ricebags and similar profundities, also seek Wisdom. Beating myself over the head as there's no-one else to do it except for one crow who drops the odd spud from a great height. It must be the same crow come down to Kerry from Meath—there can't be two bald crows at it unless it's Elijah's ravens again. Who loves me. And wait till I tell you — jackdaws in spring have laid gifts at my feet well down one ear as even I can't face a caterpillar in the gob . . . What does it all Mean? Dust to dust. Pressed further, she was literally Not Seen For —

Housemaid's Unconnected Knee

Must
I,
taking brush
in hand,
disturb the
dust
of Here and Now
when
since in reality
(Zen)
all
is void
whereon can the dust
fall . .
All
this and Heaven too!
Cleanliness
is next to
Godliness!
they
say,
Writer . .
May
I

point out that
tomes
are traditionally dusty
and what about the
names
of spiders
Now I'm
dead,
if there's anyone up there then —
cease —
God the Great Arranger
leave mine in
peace —
just
dust.
must
you, like some
dread
Housewife of All
set your
House in Order
so relentlessly.
I liked Set,
he had an ass's
head.
A New Heaven! a New

Earth!
Death!
to be
swept
under some other well
kept
carpet
or just Up
or, with a
Frown — worse,
Down . .
minus
breath, come
shout hallelujah,
thatisifyoubelieveyour
souls
may be Brassoed
to brilliance on the rainbow
weave
of the
sleeve
of God's old
vest
to
rest
on that Glassy

Floor,
or,
thrown out with the
rest
of the
rust
and holed,
old
black
kettles
in the
nettles at the
back
door;
poor
dust
having to
settle
all over
again
and again
and
again
and

my god
possibly like the
young lady of
Spain—
ad
infinitum.

Eiléan Ní Chuilleanáin

I contemplated writing this poem for a long time before actually beginning it; I needed a poem to express my fear of death and to communicate with other people so that if I died that would not be an entirely isolated moment. Two incidents gave me a starting-point; I was returning from Rome where my father was dangerously ill and expected to die, and I really did see half of a plane at Orly airport. I looked in all the newspapers for an explanation but could not find a single reference to it. A few months later I saw a car lying on its side in the road in Dublin and recognised it as belonging to friends; I spent an anxious half hour before discovering them safe in hospital. The poem is meant to apply to all deaths and it accumulates meaning as I get older and get more acquainted with death.

Deaths and Engines

We came down above the houses
In a stiff curve, and
At the edge of Paris airport
Saw an empty tunnel
— The back half of a plane, black
On the snow, nobody near it,
Tubular, burnt-out and frozen.

When we faced again
The snow-white runways in the dark
No sound came over
The loudspeakers, except the sighs
Of the lonely pilot.

The cold of metal wings is contagious:
Soon you will need wings of your own,
Cornered in the angle where
Time and life like a knife and fork
Cross, and the lifeline in your palm
Breaks, and the curve of an aeroplane's track
Meets the straight skyline.

Images of relief:
Hospital pyjamas, screens round a bed,
A man with a bloody face
Sitting up in bed, conversing cheerfully
Through cut lips:
These will fail you some time.

One day you will find yourself alone
Accelerating down a blind
Alley, too late to stop
And you know how light your death is,
How serious the survival of the others.
You will be scattered like wreckage;
The pieces, every one a different shape
Will painfully lodge in the hearts
Of everybody who loves you.

Austin Clarke

I was attracted to the theme of the straying student, or spoiled priest which is to be found in Gaelic verse. I decided to write a poem on the subject, mentioning Salamanca and other Irish Colleges of the time so as to have a European setting. I like the poem because it is my first attempt to use the common metrical design—assonance and rhyme found in many Gaelic lines—a bb c. This first attempt meant a long struggle and, despite every effort, I was unable to keep up this pattern towards the end of the lyric. Recently I came to the conclusion that my failure was due to the prompting of the sub-conscious, for the abrupt measure at the end of the poem seems to signify the disturbed mind of the student.

The Straying Student

On a holy day when sails were blowing southward,
A bishop sang the Mass at Inishmore,
Men took one side, their wives were on the other
But I heard the woman coming from the shore:
And wild in despair my parents cried aloud
For they saw the vision draw me to the doorway.

Long had she lived in Rome when Popes were bad,
The wealth of every age she makes her own,
Yet smiled on me in eager admiration,
And for a moment taught me all I know,
Banishing shame with her great laugh that rang
As if a pillar caught it back alone.

I learned the prouder counsel of her throat,
My mind was growing bold as light in Greece;
And when in sleep her stirring limbs were shown,
I blessed the noonday rock that knew no tree:
And for an hour the mountain was her throne,
Although her eyes were bright with mockery.

They say I was sent back to Salamanca
And failed in logic, but I wrote her praise
Nine times upon a college wall in France.
She laid her hand at darkfall on my page
That I might read the heavens in a glance
And I knew every star the Moors have named.

Awake or in my sleep, I have no peace now,
Before the ball is struck,my breath has gone,
And yet I tremble lest she may deceive me
And leave me in this land, where every woman's son
Must carry his own coffin and believe,
In dread, all that the clergy teach the young.

Brian Coffey

The poem grew out of the following circumstance. I once dropped into a lecture on Japanese diaries of the 17th century, and became interested in the story of a Prince Yuki-Hira who told how he had received the Emperor's decree of banishment with immediate effect. Banishment was to Suma Bay, far from villages or homes, and the path to exile ran through a mountain pass well known to similarly placed exiles through the centuries of Japanese history. I did not know whether the Japanese speak obliquely of their Emperor as I have made Yuki-Hira speak. But I liked the suggested divinity of the issuer of commands. I have not put capital letters at the beginning of each verse. Capitals are normally used to start sentences. If each verse ended with a full stop there would be naturally an occurring capital at the start of the next verse. But for centuries the sentences of verse-pieces have carried-over many lines: see Shakespeare, see Milton. The poem Yuki-Hira has a rhythm of its own, which can be discovered by reading the verses. Its subject matter should not present any difficulty, but it is necessary to remember that any poem is an entity made out of words, and one has to give a poem an attention similar to that one gives to a conversation with a new friend.

Yuki Hira

Came then His command
that I take the mountain road to
under Whose* pleasure, in obedience.

*sic

28

The shore wind chilled through the pass
after the curling smoke of the last wood fires.
Now I drag water-pails on the shore, patient
under Whose pleasure, in obedience.

Dawn, the chrysanthemums in my garden, my house
in my garden, my life, there.
My mother weeping, gently
grey hair was blown in the autumn wind.
My father stood to bless me genuflecting,
stood as an ancestor would, with steady eyes.
Knelt at my feet my wife, covered my feet
with her hair, the wind has fallen, her hair
in her sorrow drawn curled on the path.
The nurse held up my son, my son
who awakened since. Again
the melancholy wind moved the flowers,
the dust stirred on the path. I could not stay,
I could not stay the dust curled on the path.

Was gone then by the mountain road
meeting the autumn wind the shore wind
in the pass, gone
to drag water-pails on the shore, wind blowing
the sand, the chrysanthemums, the wood-fires,
the traveller's coat in the pass, patient
under Whose pleasure, in obedience.
Should any ask news.

Anthony Cronin

When you read a poem of your own again after the passage of time you often find that although you can still, more or less, approve of everything else, one vital ingredient seems to have mysteriously faded and let down the rest, as did something in the chemicals used to print old photographs. The vital ingredient is the truth.

I am glad to say that I find the feeling here still honest; if the truths are situation truths, they are honest to the situation; and the psychological generalisations are O.K. The end may be regarded as a sort of tender grace and favour statement, like the end of a Shakespearean sonnet and the fellow doesn't of course say that what he feels now to be true is absolutely so, only that he feels like that. If I am supposed to praise the poem I can only say that I like the way it moves — from line to line and from stanza to stanza; and that the way the thought is developed, sonnet-wise, is nice.

Realities

The possibilities that taunted childhood —
Step over distance and put back the clock,
I didn't mean it so it didn't happen —
Remembered afterwards return to mock

On Sunday evenings when we age most quickly
Such little livings as we ever earn,
And much bad weather falls before we really
Say with conviction what we're forced to learn:

That time is independent and that objects
Occupy space as they've a right to do,
That even on mirrored afternoons and wishes
Of any I depend as well on you;

And that a you is circumstance as real
As time or money or an act of State,
That circling in much circumstance we puzzle
Each other with a new and double fate.

All this I've learned and yet deny this evening,
And, for apology, can only plead
Contagion of your innocence restoring
The child's belief that all we need is need.

Seamus Deane

The main image in the poem is reminiscent of one used by Swift when he was lamenting his fate, cut off in Ireland from preferment in England. In a way I use the image in a converse fashion, since the Roots of the title are specifically Irish roots. Part of the poem's ambition is to indicate that growing-up and therefore away from one's roots necessarily involves a certain loss. The poem tries to communicate this sense of loss by a number of simple oppositions: e.g. older/younger; roots/top; growing/stop. The basic notion is that in drawing strength from one's roots, one can also be trapped by them; but in releasing ourselves from them, one suffers the fate that Swift referred-to—madness—the disease he described as one in which a man dies downward like a tree.

Roots

Younger,
I felt the dead
Drag at my feet
Like roots
And at every step
I heard them
Crying
Stop.

Older,
I heard the roots
Snap. The crying
Stopped. Ever since
I have been
Dying
Slowly
From the top.

Paul Durcan

When I wrote this piece I had in mind to attempt a brief note in phenomenological ontology — to use Sartre's rather awkward but precise nomenclature. More explicitly I had in mind a link-up — a synoptic transfigurative link-up — between the de la Wod Theory of the Limit of Endurance (Selskar 1832) with the 1962 O'Neill/Moriarty report from the Tivoli Laboratory at Moyvane, Texas, on the so-called Lunar Two-Fold. I wrote the piece over a period of three months in 1962.

That was ten years ago. In terms of reaction to the piece, I have had little or no reaction — as is frequently the case in the somewhat one-track world of verse. In fact the only reaction I got was, curiously enough, from a couple of members of the medical profession.

Animus, anima, amen

He went into a bar, fell deeply in love with a
        strange girl, and said:

        Where did you come from?
        The moon.
        I bet *he* didn't like that.
        Who?
        Him.
        Who's him?
        The man . . .
        In the bloody moon. Why didn't you say so?
        Katherine.
        Paul.

And he smiled. And she smiled. And they
relaxed in each other's presence for about
a year or so. In the end, she went back
to the fellow in the bloody moon.

Kevin Faller

*Years later, when I had grown up, I discovered the picture
— mentioned in this poem — wrapped in paper and found it no
longer caused me anguish.*

Blackbird

My bird is come again
and sings to me
of how my mother
died in agony
where Jesus from
a picture smiled
his heart a-glow

all warms me now
the colder that I grow

Padraic Fallon

The poem 'Weir Bridge' records a nostalgic visit to the well-known bridge and salmon weir in Galway city. As a schoolboy I often hung about the bridge during the midday break from school.

Weir Bridge

The lodestoned salmon, hurtling
Always in the right direction, find
The trickle of their birth,
Stand fantailed on the falls,
And somersault into the milting weather.

Whole gravels are in rut;
The ocean has come home to melt away
The salt, to lie beneath
A maybush and almost tenderly
Suck from the lazy heavens a blue-green fly.
   On love's seething house,
Rocking the thousand cradles, the first fresh
Will fall, and the spent bulls
Drop with it down the slow river spirals;
Aching for space now for the once rampant males;

Caught here in their bored
Congregations, while the wandering nerve
Twitches towards Norway. How many years
Since I first saw the stones waver,
The river paving turn to fins and tails,

Loafing a lunch-hour in the sun?
And here's the wheel come round again,
So much to do, so little done;
The tiny trickle of my birth
Dwindling back into the earth.

Robert Farren

Of course I have written many religious poems, poems of a believer. The motto of my first book as the Psalmist's Credidi, ergo locutus sum: I believed, therefore I have spoken.

Belief, expressed in verse, has not endeared me to many of my fellow Irish fellow-poets. But shall we not all have our say, believers and disbelievers?

Heaven, in Wordsworth's line may 'Lie about us in our infancy, but which of us—believers or disbelievers—has ever heard a sermon about Heaven will be accounted to me as presumption. So be it. I thought it worth whatever effort I could make—and I think I wrote the poem after reading those lovely seventeenth-century Anglican poets, George Herbert, and particularly Henry Vaughan, who wrote these lines about Heaven:

> They have all gone into the world of light
> And I alone sit lingering here

and, more importantly, meant them—meant that, like St. Paul, he longed to be dissolved and to be with Christ.

The Cool Gold Wines of Paradise

The God who had such heart for us
as made Him leave His house,
come down through archipelagos
of stars and live with us
has such a store of joys laid down
their savours will not sour:
the cool gold wines of Paradise,
the bread of Heaven's flour.

He'll meet the soul which comes in love
and deal it joy on joy—
as once He dealt out star and star
to garrison the sky,
to stand there over rains and snows
and deck the dark of night—
so, God will deal the soul, like stars,
delight upon delight.

Night skies have planet-armies, still
the blue is never full;
rich, massive stars have never bowed
one cloudbed's flock of wool;
red worlds of dreadful molten fire
have singed no speck of air:—
all is in place, and, each to each,
God's creatures show his care.

The soul will take each joy He deals
as skies take star on star,
be never filled, be never bowed,
be airy, as clouds are,
burn with enlarging heat and shine
with ever-brightening ray,
joyful and gathering thirst for joy
throughout Unending Day.

Padraic Fiacc

Writing this poem was like Picasso's I don't search I find.
*It dedicated itself to my American Belfast-born brothers, fellow
'Fenian Gets'. Idea-gleaming words came of themselves: our
Ulster's womb* small, black as mouse-shit, *the Ulster usage of
the word* Christian — *Protestant only. The paranoiac
dereliction of the Lower Shankill Road poor* man, the beast of
burden. *The black mood conveyed in his 'Not an inch'
contagious ergo tragically mutual* Ourselves Alone *and the
readiness to destroy the womb, the mother (like Deirdre) rather
than be born into the reality of having to change etc...*

*With another anti-war soldier poem, this poem was
published, aptly enough on July 11 (1970)—eve of the Twelfth
and* Soldier Day *in the Republic.*

A Christian Soldier Song

(For my brothers Brian and Rory)

Kings in business suits light torches at
My shrivelled up in worm-grip
Of the old rag-and-bone man won
Bowler hat myth womb of 'Not

An inch' of 'Ourselves Alone'

Womb small as a mice-dropping black
Beats the skin-tight drum
An imp-thumping whack down

Stretching over the shoulder
The bad soldier looking back:

Butcher and bread man in the rain
In funeral march for dead gain

Wear on our shirt sleeves the pain

In the Man on the mountain overlooking
                                    the waste
Who wept for man, the beast of burden

Suffering to come on to Him

Blind, cock-horse riding
Children all, all hiding

But cannot snuggle in the womb.

Monk Gibbon

Rilke says somewhere that the poet's first and indeed only business is to praise. It is not so easy in these times but—with an image of Collinstown in my mind and of the beaches in the west of Ireland from which the regretful departing visitor has perhaps come—I wrote this poem two or three years ago, laid it aside, forgot it completely, and now exhume it because it is something of antidote to our prevailing angst.

Acceptance of an epoch

I have no regrets. Some of my successors in verse,
Flinging defiance in the teeth of a world which they
hate,
Help only to stress it: they are like posters on a poetic
hoarding
As we drive out of the past into the future, to the
airport
Where the plane waits, whose engines may yet drop
off in flames,
Ready to take us to God alone knows where.

But there are still green fields and wide beaches.
I have been on them.
I remember we ran barefoot, played irresponsible
games,
Were led to expect warm sand extending for miles,
Headlands fields, brown furrows and the faint tang of
seaweed.
On these let the mind rest. They are as real as
newsprint.
And, since they taught me to love them, I salute my
predecessors.

Seamus Heaney

Two years ago I was asked to submit a committed poem to an English publication and the one I sent was Servant Boy. The poem is a literal picture of a moment in the life of a hired labourer, moving through the winter farmyard before daylight: I had in mind an old man I used to know called Ned Thompson, who hired out for years to different masters. I should like to think that it has an umbilical link with traditional songs such as The Rocks of Bawn.

> My shoes they are well worn now,
> My stockings they are thin,
> My heart is always trembling
> For fear that I might give in . . .

The man in the poem is a shadowy representative of aspects of my own experience, and also, I hope, a dramatization of the psychology of a minority or a colonised people—think how African or Indian or American Negro servants became boys once they are subject of white Anglo-Saxon domination. There is something gracious in the servant boy's quiet survival of himiliating conditions, there is something less admirable in his expert obeisance.

Servant boy

He is wintering out
the back-end of a bad year,
swinging a hurricane-lamp
through some outhouse;

a jobber among shadows.
Old work-whore, slave-
blood, who stepped fair-hills
under each bidder's eye

and kept your patience
and your counsel, how
you draw me into
your trail. Your trail

broken from haggard to stable,
a straggle of fodder
stiffened on snow,
comes first-footing

the back doors of the little
barons: resentful
and impenitent,
carrying the warm eggs.

John Hewitt

This sonnet was written at the beginning of December 1968, but the original experience had occurred early one morning in September 1934 in the street below our hotel-window in Paris where my wife and I were staying. During the intervening years 'the idea' had never offered itself as a possible poem, and for ten days before the writing of it and for a fortnight after I was not visited by any other verse. It may be, although I cannot be positive, that I had some months or weeks earlier read the essay by the Art Historian, Erwin Panofsky, entitled 'Et in Arcadia: Poussin and the Elegiac Tradition'.

A surprise for me, outside my more usual logically-ordered, low-charged descriptive manner, I enjoyed the tricks it seemed to play with the sonnet-form in its shuttling back and forth in time against the orthodox armature of the three-quatrains and the closing couplet. I was pleased with the run of internal rhymes, played, splay, strayed; classic, pastoral; beside, tideless; and with the assonances and alliterations—every single line threaded with one or more sibilants like a sustained whisper and by the contrast of the quiet-back-street in a busy city with the unpeopled Mediterranean shores, although Greece, the police-state of the usurping Colonels,* and Sicily, once the home-ground of Theocritus, is now the island of the Mafia and that brave reformer Danilo Dolci—circumstances which give a dash of irony to the Idyll convention.

When, a couple of years ago, I read in a Sunday newspaper Hemingway's account of the same piping goatherd, I realised with deep satisfaction that my memory had not played me false. I have, I believe, written better, perhaps more popular poems, but this has a unique place in my affection, a self-contained, precious moment in my shared past, something given, not earned.

---

*Happily, changed since. [Ed.]

Et tu in Arcadia vixisti

You woke me, rising—this in Paris once—
I watched you stepping—thirty years ago—
to the long windows,—Many such we've since
unshuttered back from other streets below,
but on no more than stir of wheel or foot—
as, finger-signalled, following, I stood
beside you, hearing, drifting-up, a flute-
like music, blown through the clean hollow wood,
as, leaning, a dark lad, against the wall,
played to the splay of goats about his knees,
strayed, so it seemed, from classic pastoral,
an instant's magic—never ours in Greece,
when, later, older—or in Sicily—
we stood, at dawn, beside the tideless sea.

Pearse Hutchinson

Elegies and love-poems are the hardest to write well. The good elegies you can count on your hands; I choose this poem because I think it nearly works, even though it's both a love-poem of a kind, and as near to an elegy as I've so far achieved, an elegy both in prospect and retrospect—though unwittingly: it was written about my mother when she was 79, a year before she died.

Like trees, like islands

Kneel to fasten your shoes.
Kneel, creaking, clicking.
We seem near.

Blade, thong, buckle.
Knew by which notch
takes easy entry
how swollen, how tired, how rested.
How near we seem—like trees, like islands.
Like trees on their neighbouring islands
that cannot uproot themselves and walk—
no kneeling fingers—
on water to meet. But moved
by an occasional strong wind
they touch branches, tangle, may even
break each other. As long
as life, the heart tholes.
They knew, in a way then, how near
their islands are. Swap nests.
Trunk-tug is too strong
for any thong not to give soon,
The meeting lasts only a minute,
but these minutes recur,
and in that minute the trees congress
their different bird-song, squirrels, iguanas,
climbing, swarming, crawling life,
fruits and flowers if any.
They can even share lightning.

I kneel to fasten your shoes.
We seem near.

Valentin Iremonger

This is a very recent poem (1971) less personal than is usual with one, but perhaps advancing middle age brings an additional quota of objective gloom even to a poet never noted for any degree of high spirits in his work.

The master plan

In the beginning
You lie on your back,
Eyes closed,
Arms tentatively moving,
An occasional cry.

Later, tossing and turning
For many years,
You wonder at the apparently
Haphazard movements of life,
Of nature, of joys,
Of griefs, humiliations,
Of memories too many to count.

In the end
You lie on your back,
Eyes closed,
Arms over chest stilled,
No cry at all.

John Jordan

The occasion of these verses was a sentimental pilgrimage to the birthplace of Santa Teresa, foundress of the Reformed or Discalced Carmelites. This visit coincided with celebrations of the 35th anniversary of Franco's usurpation in 1936. Hence the magnificent display of fireworks, which I have tried to describe. Earlier that day I had been reading a biography of Teresa by a pietistic and bad rococo writer called Füllop-Miller where I noted that the great Doctor Teresa did not scruple to accept gold plundered by her conquistador brother. 'Discalced' of course means 'without shoes'.

Second Thoughts

Ascending descending
in ethereal verbena
swallows dip wings
to jazzed-up 'pases'
light, light guerdon
kisses o kisses peach
the stone ochre stone
of the Church of San Pedro.
In the Holy City of Avila

Coruscating syncopating
ebonite blackness
factitious stars emerald
ruby grenadine
mantillas in apple
waterfalls in silver
pluming smoke palm-trees
odour of cordite.
In the Holy City of Avila

O what a squall
sent the Sierra
chair hooked table
glass ticked off bottle
little ones ululated
old ones castigated
flight of the innocents
denser the plumage of
'The Eagle of Gredos'
In the Holy City of Avila

And I curse the turgid
Rene-Füllop Miller
easier not to know
plundered New World gold
paid the last builders' bills
for the Convent of San José.
Did Teresa ever give a damn
for the discalced Indian?
In the Holy City of Avila

55

Trevor Joyce

No comment to offer.

Twin Relative Deposition

2 years of watches remark the end of autumn

Subtle as the leaking stench of gas
that trembles the slight web of sleep
they died; and so quick the dead
lost their composure, moulting age with face,
all habit broken and all gesture discontinued.

The dandelion, frost-quenched, watches in the house.
marks time along the well-path; lion's-tooth
that emptied check and jaw of meat,
hiding in the hollow house now, waiting
near the well where the neighbours don't go now.

Soon even the memory will be gone,
the old woman and her brother will be a broken habit
the neighbours will compose new plots;
the well-path will be overgrown;
well forgotten, covered by a policy of growth.

Lion's-tooth, famished at the acrid lakeside,
re-mounts to the village as the mercury drops:

oil bright in a crock,
    flame tilting at the wick;
        blue-herons in a bladed bay.

                last autumn month.

Richard Kell

I don't think I have a favourite poem, but Arches is one of those I have continued to like. Why? Partly for the extraneous reason that it came whole and quickly and didn't need a lot of revision. More importantly, it expresses what may be a psychological truth—or at any rate asks a serious question about personality—in a way that pleases me. There is a small argument given entirely in images, and the meaning focusses clearly as soon as it is discovered. Apart from its logical implications, however, I like to think that the image of the bridge over water has some of the intrinsic vitality of a symbol or a true metaphor—that it shines with its own light, so to speak, even when the riddle has been solved. Lastly, the poem has a fairly definite external shape—matching the internal shape, the shape of the meaning—without being rigidly metrical: if there is such a thing as freedom within order, this, I hope, is a tiny example of it.

Arches

Arches on land,
half-circles only,
might dream
of what they miss.

And yet to stand
in a dark stream,
is this
not twice as lonely?

Brendan Kennelly

This poem deals with a favourite theme of mine: the recurring sense of loss and inadequacy in a time of apparent fulfilment. One state emphasizes the other. Indeed, so closely are the two conditions linked, one might say that one state is the other. So I wanted to suggest this disturbing approximation, this inexplicable link, this leap from gaiety to desolation. It strikes me that the poem moves from a dancing room to a weeping wall, from images of delight to images of decay. I would like to make it clear that delight and decay are most real to me when they too are dancing together, locked in a blood-rhythm, seen vividly in the contrast of each other. That is my truest feeling about them. They grope towards each other in aspiration and conflict. And they do this endlessly, in my own heart.

Something is missing

Something is missing
Even when we all dance together
In a noisy ring

About the house.
When the loved ones come
with their joyous

Voices and faces
And the dreary season throws away its grief
And every room rejoices

With light and laughter.
What is that moment
In the middle of it all

When more and more gaiety is born
As though each hour were a womb
To bring some happiness forth?

Something is missing
So laugh till the walls shake
Like old men holding their sides

In case the fit might split a rib
And hurry them down the road
To a damp place

Of gravelled paths, coarse grass,
Gates stuck in their hinges
And crass ravenous moss

Creeping
Along the walls
Stained with weeping.

Thomas Kinsella

Chosen not necessarily as the best I think I have written, but as the one of best-directed anger—anger at the continuum of waste, injustice, etc., in which we are apparently expected to survive.

Ballydavid pier

Noon. The luminous tide
Climbs through the heat, covering
Grey shingle. A film of scum
Searches first among litter,
Cloudy with (I remember)
Life; then crystal-clear shallows
Cool on the stones, silent
With shells and claws, white fish bones;
Farther out a bag of flesh,
Foetus of goat or sheep
Wavers below the surface.

62

Allegory forms of itself:
The line of life creeps upward
Replacing one world with another,
The welter of its advance
Sinks down into clarity,
Slowly the more foul
Monsters of loss digest . . .

Small monster of true flesh
Brought forth somewhere
In bloody confusion and error
And flung into bitterness,
Blood washed white:
Does that structure satisfy?

The ghost tissue hangs unresisting
In allegorical waters,
Lost in self-search
— a swollen blind brow
Humbly crumpled over
Budding limbs, unshaken
By the spasms of birth or death.

The Angelus, faint bell-notes
From some church in the distance
Tremble over the water.
It is nothing. The vacant harbour
Is filling; it will empty.
The misbirth touches the surface
And glistens like quicksilver.

James Liddy

This extract is from a serial poem, A Munster Song of Love and War ... A theme of the poem is the magnificent ambivalence of the figure of Michael Collins, not just in patriotism but in folklore. I want his face, his swagger, what he may have said, to be as interesting and maybe as menacing as Dean Swift is in the files of The Folklore Commission.

The new O'Dwyer's dim lights. "You hate
me" by the wallpaper
"We don't hate the English" buckling off
Our swords we dream past
War.
I saw
Gleaming host locked with me upon the narrow plain
where
None see past love.
I dound myself alone
(Where was yellow haired Donough?)
Fighting for our wild our bleak island.

Michael Longley

I wrote this poem in August 1968 after nearly two years in the wilderness. I had been finding it difficult to write naturally and well: none of the skills I had acquired over the previous decade seemed valid. From time to time during this barren period I tried to produce a piece on the English poet, John Clare, whom I greatly admire. I accumulated a large pile of notes, half-lines, phrases, bits and pieces about him: but my words always sounded lifeless. I shelved the project for several months; then one evening in Dublin when I least expected it and when I was without my notes and preliminary sketches, the poem I had laboured for so long to bring into being presented itself very quietly and with little effort—I wrote it out more or less as it stands now. The earlier disappointments get into the lines, I think: it is, to some extent a poem about not being able to write a poem or, at least, about having had to live for too long without the benediction of words working properly together. Perhaps it is disenchanted rather than disappointed: I like to think it has earned the muted optimism of the last few lines. But more than anything else this poem tries to salute a great man. Clare's gentleness of spirit corrected my ambition and will, dictated the pace of my imagination, and generously in the end gave me a poem which, after four years, I am still fond of and grateful for.

Journey Out Of Essex

or, John Clare's Escape from the Madhouse

I am lying with my head
Over the edge of the world,
Unpicking my whereabouts
Like the asylum's name
That they stitch on the sheets.

Sick now with bad weather
Or a virus from the fens,
I dissolve in a puddle
My biographies of birds
And the names of flowers.

That they may recuperate
Alongside the stunned mouse,
The hedgehog rolled in leaves,
I am putting to bed
In this rheumatic ditch

The boughs of my harvest-home,
My wives, one on either side,
And keeping my head low as
A lark's nest, my feet toward
Helpston and the pole star.

Seán Lucy

Even though a reasonably intelligent acquaintance once told me that he didn't understand a word of it, I still hope this poem explains itself, or rather displays itself, fairly clearly. Accepting sleep is accepting death 'What is terrible for us,' says de Chardin, 'is to be cut off from things through some inward diminishment that can never be retrieved.' (Le Milieu Divin). Against this dread we may set the deep intuition of sleep, of 'letting go', as the only hope of grace: the sleep of King Lear or of the sailors and others in The Tempest.

Fear of sleep

He didn't like the thought of letting go.
Disturbed by darkness, he resented sleep;
Slept soon nevertheless, slept well moreover,
Rolling the slack mind in that tidal deep.

Black over grey, the lines between his days, the
monoliths of night troubled his mind:
"Where was I when the empty clock struck three?
"Distant? Or nonexistent? Merely deaf and blind?"

Terrified of losing maximum consciousness,
Of precious self perished forever, he wept;
Prayed to the god of light for consolation;
And found that consolation only when he slept.

The forest of doze spreads its dark blue branches,
Seas of slumber run green to black deep.
Into those profunditites the heart swings down its
    anchors.
The sailors rest. Music. Pure sleep.

Brian Lynch

I have always been inclined to believe that poetry, apart from being a mystery, was saying simply what you most wanted to say. Intensity and concentration will get anyone through.

This piece describes things I'd seen or thought about my father's death. My father was fairly young when he died and so he was suddenly overtaken as if from hiding and he became as old as anyone can be. It must have been there all along. The other things can be seen by anyone, they are phenomena (but the connections I make are personal)—gravestones, say, get covered with moss stains that are a bit like the freckles on old skin; and nails do grow. Maybe I didn't know that when I was nine.

I was sad and unhappy and ignorant about death but I learned something about it which in a secret way I thought no one else knew, not those of my own age nor those who were older, teachers for instance—death was real and it killed people.

The last lines are a bit more difficult for me to understand. Sometimes I had very bright dreams that my father was alive. And so waking was painful. But that also was when I found out a bit more about love.

If this were a real poem you'd recognise it.

For My Father

When my father died
Age seeped out of his bones
Age that hid under flaps
Closed his eyes and tightened
His skin to coarse leather
Marbled as gravestones
With the freckles of age
While his moustache
Comic Hitler in life
Continued to grow for some hours
His nails growing
Into my eyes and soul.

I was nine at the time
Put on age like a suit
Watched from the mountains
Our city in the sun
With the most melancholy
Ignorant eye of youth on death
And learned so soon
That dream of love asleep
In the painful morning visions
Of our true undying fathers.

James McAuley

As a general rule, I let the subject dictate, or at least suggest, the form of a poem. This is the best excuse I can give right now for the fact that most of my recent poems run fairly long by lyric cry standards. And I have got myself into trouble in scholastic circles for my nasty comments on the cult of the skinny lyric that whinges down the page in two-word lines.

The poems that do stay under or around twenty lines are amenable to nervous little tricks of metre and rhyme, which makes me covertly proud of them, as of a child who says something unexpectedly witty.

In recent times, I've been inclined to write about immediate preoccupations, veering from the erotic to what my wife calls my apocalypse poems: signifying perhaps a long dry spell, since I count only twenty poems or so in the past two years.

Veterans' Supper is, I suppose, one of my apocalypse poems; I would prefer to let the little beast have its own growl.

Veterans' Supper

The men for the occasion had set up
The trestle tables like barricades beneath
Heroic yellowing portraits; and paper cups
Were brought by wives and widows, and neat

Well-seasoned pots of home-cooked rations rose
Like batteries strategically placed
Round the tables, so all comers could choose
A little of everything, according to their tastes.

The Ladies' Auxiliary strove all afternoon
In the heat of Independence Day to make
A homely atmosphere in the barracks room
Where the veterans met weekly for old times' sake

And in the evening, as the sun burned down
In scathing orange over the shady streets,
And festive rockets crackled and flared round the
    town,
The veterans and their families came to eat,

Trooping past the tables, filling their paper plates
With succulent vittles, paying their dollar fees;
Then, armed with plastic forks, they sat and ate
Their cornmeal, tacos, sauerkraut, rice, macaroni
    cheese.

Roy McFadden

I was reared in a Belfast suburb called Knock (the Chinatown referred-to in my poems in The Garryowen *). The triangle was a recently suburbanised townland, still rural and squirish in parts. Stringer's Field was the residual grounds of a stately house, almost a wood under whose trees we played Sherwood games of Robin Hood and innocent gappy-toothed Maid Marion made, more often than not, to queen her part, until, Marion apart, we became citizens in Baden Powell uniforms.*

My family left the townland-suburb shortly after the start of the last war; and only long after that vast crater of missing years did it occur to me to look for hints and flints of myself when I used to trespass in Stringer's Field now a guilty blush of redbrick villas with identical cars outside identical doors. Those streets were made for a horse-and-cart. Nostalgia in a car is a contradiction in terms of Chinatown.

Stringer's field

This is no proper route for middle-age
Briefed with honour cards from sunday school,
Key lacking door, superior car too big
For the meagre streets of Kick-the-can and Tig.

I have gone back too far. Then a townland,
Before the first death, brimmed and hummed with
    summer
And life like loafing kerbstones stretched eternal
And The News was always the same from wireless and
    journal

I have gone back too far. Then that white summer
Trite with daisies and that next-door girl's
Buttercup kiss through the laurels when we were seven
And at night the streetlamp guttering up to heaven,

My robining boyhood under Stringer's trees:
Now, leafed back, reveals the kerbstones cold,
Kiss blown, ironic laurels unallayed
By my return to all I left unsaid.

James McKenna

A personal loss the more grievous when seen through an actual ironical situation regarding the reckless haphazard art patronage, heightened finally by the Ulster tragedy as it unfolds. The artist called upon to be everything—but an artist. Whereas he had hardly been thought of before—even as a human being.

Summer in Dublin 1969

We spent all summer
in this city;
put on little plays;
opened a gallery;
spoke on art and the people—
whilst people strangely
kept going away.
For this we swabbed our affliction
in yet more work.

And when the fury broke
to the North East
we were called on
to cry out loud:
why justice was not being done,
and to do all we could,
lacking arms and money
to be seen
to be concerned.

Now with autumn
a call for culture comes
in a manner unlikely
to bring us hope,
or make our well being
a burden upon this city;
a city of culture
attending to its own.

Tom McLoughlin

This poem is an intimation of future loneliness, of the death of a friendship—a weak-kneed feeling that I will never be able to survive alone, a self-piteous confession of affection and dependence. I prefer it to other more stiff-lipped poems of mine because it recognises and at the same time embraces and expresses that whingeing self-pity which, I feel, is basic to my temperament.

Although many of the words and phrases used may be commonplace and banal, that doesn't seem so important to me. My thoughts usually take shape in such language; so, better that, than any 'vivid original diction' which is not my own.

In ten years of less

I'll come to meet you at some cold airport,
Your wife still on a leash—just one bright kid.
'Time can't make that much difference'. But it did,
We're different people now, we're poles apart.
Travelling from strength to strength, you have decided
On poets of whom I've never even heard;
My lack of purpose grew this foolish beard,
Big hopes too heavy on me, I subsided
Back to the hometown with my cooing wife
And cried the lack of everything—of you.
I didn't have courage to pursue
The jagged rhythms of a brave new life.

Here's not what's left but what was always me,
And you, live, lucid, burning energy.

Derek Mahon

This poem started off as a comment on a photograph of Mûnch's studio in Oslo which appeared in one of the Sunday colour supplements a couple of years back. Mûnch was something of a recluse in his later years, a valetudinarian artist of the Proustian variety who kept to his room most of the time. One thinks of him doing little besides working and sleeping. The studio photograph connected for me with a phrase in a review by Beckett of a Jack Yeats exhibition: The being in the room when it happens in the street, the being in the street when it happens in the room, *a phrase which originally stood as epigraph to the poem. The phrase in turn suggested the oblique, and possibly escapist, relationship of the Artist to his historical circumstances, particularly where those circumstances include a violent and complex political upheaval. The poem became a refusal to write a war poem—if you prefer, an assertion of the necessarily private nature of a certain kind of artistic activity. Even so, by reference to the ideally timeless aspects of art, it does, I think, make a kind of historical comment—to the effect, perhaps, that in the brief working and sleeping existence where the art is done we (and the art) are bound by the conditions of that existence. The artist is bound by the nature of paint, everyone by the facts of life.*

Edvard Mûnch

You would think with so much going on outside
The deal table would make for the window,
The ranged crockery freak and wail
Remembering its dark origins, the frail
Oilcloth, in a fury of recognitions,
Disperse in a thousand directions,
And the simple bulb in the ceiling, honed
By death to a worm of pain, to a hair
Of heat, to a light snowflake laid
In a dark river at night (and wearied
Above all by the life-price of time
And the failure by only a few tenths
Of an inch but completely and for ever
Of the ends of a carefully drawn equator
To meet, sing and be one) abruptly
Roar into the floor.

           But it
Never happens like that. Instead
There is this quivering silence
In which, day by day, the play
Of light and shadow (shadow mostly)
Repeats itself, though never exactly.

This is the all-purpose bed-, work—and bedroom.
Its mourning faces are cracked porcelain only quicker,
Its knuckles doorknobs only lighter,
Its occasional cries of despair
A function of the furniture.

John Montague

I comply, while registering a protest: I have no particular favourite among my poems, and do not feel I should have, any more than a father should choose among his children. But I am aware that certain poems sail away, as though they had a life of their own, and All Legendary Obstacles seems to be one. I took ten years to write it; that is, the original experience was in '56 but it was not until I returned to teach in the area a decade later that I dared to explore it. What pleases me is that, on the one hand, the poem re-discovers a pattern of myth — which one I will leave the reader to find out, but that black porter, and the old woman did not appear by accident — and, on the other, it is rigorously faithful to the details of the experience; I found I remembered the names of the trains, as bright as yesterday. Another thing: All Legendary Obstacles cannot be pigeonholed as an Irish poem — it is a poem by an Irishman about one of the most moving experiences of his life. Last time out, it was in a programme of American poetry, which is as it should be: the truth of poetry is as exact as that of science, although more secret, and it ignores frontiers. The ideal reader would not be an Irishman or an American, but someone under the sway of love.

All Legendary Obstacles

All legendary obstacles lay between
Us. the long imaginary plain,
The monstrous ruck of mountains
And, swinging across the night,
Flooding the Sacramento, San Joaquin,
The hissing drift of winter rain.

All day I waited, shifting
Nervously from station to bar
As I saw another train sail
By, the San Francisco Chief or
Golden Gate, water dripping
From great flanged wheels.

At midnight you came, pale
Above the negro porter's lamp.
I was too blind with rain
And doubt to speak, but
Reached from the platform
Until our chilled hands met.

You had been travelling for days
With an old lady, who marked
A neat circle on the glass
With her glove, to watch us
Move into the wet darkness
Kissing, still unable to speak.

Brian Mooney

This poem is the last in a collection, Island Awakening, *written during a nine month stay on Inis Mean in the Aran Islands. Many of the images it contains impressed themselves early on in the stay but did not finally form a coherent whole until departure. For this reason it is probably one of the more finished and mature poems of the collection.*

Leaving the Island

At first the tide nerved
through hidden channels.
I knew that the sight
of the bladders of seaweed,
like ballcocks rising,
would cause a shrill, uneasy stirring
among the birds.

Knots are dapper fishers.
They would pipe to each other
in their own excited morse
through the air's awning
as the sea tipped their pools.
The fresh-water spring
would have stopped its blathering
before the land locked.

A man draped with ribbonweed
was making his way
slowly back from the rocks;
the birds were coming in flocks;
and lapwing waved
their idiotic semaphore
as the first breaker
tore on the shore.

Paul Muldoon

The characters in this poem are fictitious and any resemblance to persons living or dead is accidental. People can just as easily live at the edge of an event and be somehow implicated, in Ireland as in the America of the Civil War.

The Field Hospital

Taking, giving back their lives
By the strength of our bare hands,
By the silence of our knives,
We answer to no grey South

Nor blue North, not self defence,
The lie of just wars, neither
Cold nor hot blood's difference
In their discharging of guns,

But that hillside of fresh graves.
Would this girl brought to our tents
From whose flesh we have removed
Shot that George, on his day off,

Will use to weigh fishing lines,
Who died screaming for ether,
Yet protest our innocence?
George lit the lanterns, in danced

Those gigantic, yellow moths
That brushed right over her wounds,
Pinning themselves to our sleeves
Like medals given the brave.

Donal Murphy

When I was growing up in Cork City, the upland region in the north of that county where my father was born had an almost Biblical remoteness about it. We had no living relatives near the ancestral mountain which I call Duarigle in this poem, so I never visited those 'Faraway' highlands where the River Blackwater rises.

My eventual discovery of the area was not as a tourist on a sentimental journey, but as a Civil Engineer engaged in riverine studies for the Department of Agriculture and Fisheries.

In the poem, I look on the landscape with a dual but integrated vision, seeing the valley where my father was born, both as the cradle of a river which is the lifestream of the whole region, and as a kind of Jehoshaphat where I will join my rugged ancestors on the day of General Judgement.

Blackwater Valley

Knock twice upon this rock:
Once, with the rod of Aaron, knock for water.
Duarigle's black head strains to the sky
And sucks the trailing udder of a cloud.
Below, long in the sun, sparkles the valley
Traced by a line of water.

Knock now for blood.
I see the people standing in the valley
Queueing in generations for the judgement:
Patient, immobile figures
Carved from the gritstone of the hills round them.
The mountain sunlight
Glints from the raindrops on the weathered faces.

Hayden Murphy

To write of one's relationship with writing is usually the work of a critic, to write of one's reaction to political situations is usually the work of a historian: Pablo Neruda the poetic and critical historian of Chile has managed to combine these occupations into a form of art only capable to the prophet or the poet. It is sitting beside his poems with those words 'I am a guitar' echoing in my mind that I, writing as I, wonder at my own audaciousness and yet feel confident enough to raise my voice in the silence.

For Pablo Neruda

Your poems are black
but mine are grey
with the paring,
useless tearing, of meaning.

Strokes of definition
sit by your fingers
to be chosen, ambidexterous i
am clumsy with my learning.

You fold a rainbow
into a sun-lit song, for me
its silence at the edge
of thunder's thumb.

Your poems sing
but mine can only hum, you
TREAT your words, i argue
and they leave me.

Richard Murphy

The Reading Lesson had two starting points: one in private experience, the other in classical myth. On the surface it concerns a boy, an illiterate—who grew up as a tinker in a wattle tent on the roadside, learning to read. Undercurrents of his problem go back into mythological time. At this level, the poem concerns Hermes, the messenger of heaven; god of eloquence, science and commerce; inventor of the lyre and the alphabet; god of the roads who protected travellers; a divine charmer and a thief. Not for him, though, the sweat of reading and writing books, arts of a much more settled laborious agrarian divinity. Added to this is the teacher's ironical tension, trying to liberate the boy by education, while envying him his freedom that goes with his wild nomadic refusal to learn.

The Reading Lesson

Fourteen years old, learning the alphabet,
He finds letters harder to catch than hares
Without a greyhound. Can't I give him a dog
To track them down, or put them in a cage?
He's caught in a trap, until I let him go,
Pinioned by "Don't you want to learn to read?"
"I'll be the same man whatever I do".

He looks at a page as a mule balks at a gap
From which a goat may hobble out and bleat.
His eyes jink from a sentence like flushed snipe
Escaping shot. A sharp word, and he'll mooch
Back to his piebald mare and bantam cock.
Our purpose is as tricky to retrieve
As mercury from a smashed thermometer.

2
"I'll not read any more". Should I give up?
His hands, long-fingered as a Celtic scribe's,
Will grow callous, gathering sticks or scrap;
Exploring pockets of the horny drunk
Loiterers at the fairs, giving them lice.
A neighbour chuckles. "You can never tame
The wild-duck: when his wings grow, he'll fly off".

If books resemble roads, he'd quickly read:
But they're small farms to him, fenced by the page,
Ploughed into lines, with letters drilled like oats:
A field of tasks he'll always be outside.
If words were bank-notes, he would filch a wad;
If they were pheasants, they'd be in his pot
For breakfast, or if wrens he'd make them king.

Paul Murray

A poem, because it is a sign, must attempt to recreate the real presence of its object. When that presence is something violent like death or insanity, how is this possible? Almost inevitably the poet distorts the real for the sake of form or worse, writes platitudes. Similarly, the act of formal prayer or ritual can fail too easily in its attempt to come to terms with intractable experience and become instead an empty sign. Unless they have faith in the power of words and in the Word, the poet and the priest will turn their backs upon the real, isolated within their separate rituals.

Rites

I   This is my fear

This is my fear
that I who have observed
the beauty of an insane woman
time after time, appear
to imitate her ritual; the water
she has carried within
cupped hands,
I cannot hold. Into the thin
and delicate vessel of poetry,
live water spills.

II   None

What requiem shall the Choir sing?
Other than the need to overcome despair,
Somehow to give order to this thing,
What use our ritual? What prayer
Could exorcise ghosts buried in
The conscience of this city? At night gunpowder
Flames above the asphalt. Only the sirens sing.

Desmond O'Grady

When at Harvard, I was in the habit of taking walks on the Kelleher, Professor of Irish History and Modern Irish Literature. Irish history and literature were the subjects of our conversations. After winter, the frozen river thawed and the students would begin rowing practice. To our left stood the ivied walls of the Harvard Houses. Across in Boston towered a skyscraper.

I was reminded how, as a child in Ireland, I used to walk along the Shannon with my uncle, Feathereye Mykie while the boat clubs rowed at practice. Feathereye was a storyteller and through stories told me the myths, legends and history of Ireland on those walks. Now twenty years later, Irish-American Professor Kelleher and I were doing the same thing under different circumstances. For me, a resident alien in America, the question presented itself of how to bridge the Atlantic, how to connect the American coast of our present lives with the Irish coast of our origins. I was aware too of process—*the passage of time, a winter survived, of the ocean eroding the coasts of Europe and America.*

The two of us walking, certain images came into my head: Picasso's blue *painting of two standing acrobats with a small hound and in the background the faint outline of a house's gable; the arms of Shiva casting shadows, like the bare trees along the Charles; fields strewn with human offal after a Dionysian sacrifice. Then the two acrobats turned towards each other and engaged in a silent slow-motion struggle that resembled some primitive dance. One embodied the qualities of the Apollonian, the Classic; the other the qualities of the Dionysian, the Romantic. Out of this struggle of young and old, of Old and New a new order promised to emerge victorious. With dusk, all the shadows of the past, of history and literature, gathered for the struggle's end, to witness this*

96

*emergence. And, as in Athens, on the feast of Dionysus, after
the performance of Aeschylus' Orestia all Athenian resident
aliens who were citizens for the day and wore the saffron toga,
walked in torchlit procession up to the Parthenon and Athena's
statue, so I, a resident alien in America, walked, as the saffron
sun set, up to the University with this poem in my head, the
kind of which I had never written before and which marks the
point of development from my old methods of ordering my
chaotic experience in verse to a new, and for me, richer method.*

Professor Kelleher and the Charles River

The Charles River reaps here like a sickle. April
Light sweeps flat as ice on the inner curve
Of the living water. Overhead, far from the wave, a
   dove
White gull heads inland. The spring air, still
Lean from winter, Thaws. Walking, John
Kelleher and I talk on the civic lawn.

West, to our left, past some trees, over the ivy walls,
The clock towers, pinnacles, the pillared university
  yard.
The Protestant past of Cambridge, New England
  selfconsciously dead
In the thawing clay of the Old Burying Ground. Miles
East, over the godless Atlantic, our common brother,
Ploughing his myth-muddy fields, embodies our order.

But here, while the students row by eights and fours on
  the river—
As my father used to row on the Shannon when, still a
  child,
I'd cross Thomond Bridge every Sunday, my back to
  the walled
And turreted castle, listening to that uncle Mykie
  deliver
His version of history—I listen now to John Kelleher
Unravel the past a short generation later.

Down at the green banks nerve end, its roots half in
  the river,
A leafing tree gathers refuse. The secret force
Of the water worries away the live earth's under-
  surface
But his words, for the moment, hold back time's
  being's destroyer,
While the falling wave on both thighs of the ocean
Erodes the cost, at its dying conceptual motion.

Two men, one young, one old, stand stopped acrobats
   in the blue
Day, their bitch river to heel. Beyond
Some scraper, tower or ancestral house's gable end.
Then helplessly, as in some ancient dance, the two
   Begin their ageless struggle, while the tree's shadow
With all its arms, crawls on the offal-strewn meadow.

Locked in their mute struggle there by the blood-
   loosed tide
The two abjure all innocence, tear down pat order—
The one calm, dispassionate, clearsighted, the other
Wild with ecstasy, intoxicated, world mad.
Surely some new order is at hand,
Some new form emerging where they stand.

Dusk. The great dim tide of shadows from the past
Gathers for the end—the living and the dead.
All force is fruitful. All opposing powers combine.
Aristocratic privilege, divine sanction, anarchy at last
Yield the new order. The saffron sun sets.
All shadows procession in an acropolis of lights.

Frank Ormsby

This poem grew out of two related images; one was of furniture-strewn pavements during recent flooding in Belfast; the other, a newsreel picture of riot victims moving house. The common phrase: political climate *suggested the relationship. The Farset is the stream from which Belfast took its name—in Gaelic Beal Feirste, the mouth of the Farset—the stream which now runs beneath High Street.*

Floods

At high tide the sea is under the city,
A natural subversive. The Farset,
Forced underground, observes no curfew,
And, sleepless in their beds, the sullen drains
Move under manholes.

Blame fall on the builders, foolish men.
The strained civility of city, sea, breaks
Yearly, snapped by native rains,
Leaving in low streets the sandbagged doors,
The furnished pavements.

Basil Payne

Most poets find that after a poem in finally written it is almost a thing apart. You move on to the next poem. You may read the previous one at a poetry-reading, but the rewards are those of performance or communicating. But occasionally a poet finds that one of his own poems haunts him; acquires growing significance. It may not be his best poem,, but it is generally a poem which exists at several levels. This is such a poem. It is popular with children and adults. I have read it in schools, Universities and Cultural Centres in Dublin, Galway, Zagreb, Vienna, Zurich and Paris. In all these places the audience laughed (with fear?) during the second half.

To me, it is a tragic poem—despite its comic absurdity. ·Laughter and tears and absurdity are bed-companions. And this poem deals with a concrete situation—which strips it of all literary conceit. I would be content to be remembered by it as one of my most representative shorter poems.

Watching My Father Shaving

Watching my father shaving in the kitchen
Before a cracked mirror: this was my four-years-old
                                    highlight
In our otherwise humdrum daily domestic ritual.

Mother sliced onions, grey eyes smarting with tears,
Or, scarlet-faced, black-leaded the kitchen range;
Polished the steel parts with fine-grained emery-paper.

Later, she's doing the wash in a zinc bathtub;
Stiffens father's half-dozen shirt collars with Robin
  starch
—-Father was dapper: starched collar, bow-tie, trim
  moustache.

Watching him shaving made my intestines tighten;
My eye-balls harden with awe; my heartbeats
  quicken;
That evil steel cut-throat razor—supposing slipped

On Dad's Adam's apple. Sliced it off. Plop.
                                        Like that.
What would I do? Run out to the clothes-line
                              for mother?
Pick *it* up from the floor; stick it back on his bleeding
  throat?

It never happened, of course: silent, as ordered,
I'd watch him scrape creamy lather from his cheeks,
Chin, neck—such expertise!—then finally throat.

A daily miracle. "There now" (the razor snapped
  shut),
"I'm sure your mother could do with your help
  outside."
Between us, once more, we'd outsmarted honed-up
  tragedy.

Father died having breakfast (*from natural causes*
The Coroner's verdict recorded). My electric razor
  purrs.
My young son complains it causes T.V. interference.

Richard Ryan

John Berryman died on January 7th, 1972.

Bright sails
i.m. John Berryman

I.
Blind harper, blind
fiddler, blind poet;
old hold-alls stuffed

with rage and ragged
dreams, petty session
held in ditch and shebeen.

The wise threw bright sails
to the wind and dropped
dead in their dreams

between candle and quill,
rats at them.

II.
Like truth, over
the horizons they stumble now
like mammoths come back,

all our confused galleons
staggering in tempest,
collapsing under the weight

of their priceless cargoes;
on the rocks they flounder
toward, the girls glitter

the gifts of their bodies
opening like wounds, while again
on a far horizon the dawn

sails by like a world that works,
brown men singing in its rigging,

a golden fleet forever sailing the wrong way.

James Simmons

Firstly I like the subject, the meretricious and egocentric dreams of the young man being modified and qualified by experience until he reached an almost heroic acceptance in the last stanza, endorsing a world without him. The subject is common but of primary importance. In so far as it incorporates statement, I think the statements are wise, and the texture of language and emotion convey the appropriate richness of wisdom.

Secondly I like the extended symbol taken from the world of cinema, the most obvious source of meretricious dreams for our time. The ingredients must be almost universally familiar, so that the distinctions are easily communicable and yet exactly right. In this context the frustration of the ego is seen to be at once intense and comic.

Finally I like the diction and rhythm of the poem. The words fall naturally and yet everything is precisely ordered, cogent. Sometimes I buy order at the expense of feeling; but not often, and certainly not here. Reading it over again, I have the happy feeling that each stanza keeps a nice tension between the hunger for success and the need for acceptance.

Written, Directed-By and Starring Himself

The scripts I used to write for the young actor—
Me—weren't used. And now I couldn't play
The original parts and, as director,
I'd turn myself, if I applied, away.

My break will come; but now the star's nature
His parts need character and "love" is out.
He learns to smile on birth and death, to endure:
It's strange I keep the old scripts lying about.

Looking them over I've at times forgot
They've never been put on. I seem to spend
Too much time reading through a final shot
Where massed choirs sing, they kiss, and then THE
   END.

It's hard to start upon this middle phase
When my first period never reached the screen,
And there's no end now to my new screen-plays,
They just go on from scene to scene to scene.

The hero never hogs the screen because
His wife, his children, friends, events intrude.

When he's not on the story doesn't pause—
Not if he dies. I don't see why it should.

Michael Smith

The poem was written soon after a visit to a cancer hospital where my mother lay dying. That, simply, is the infinitely complex human background of the poem. With the death of someone you love, something of yourself also dies. Perhaps a few lines from a really great Irish poet, Mr. Brian Coffey, will serve better than anything I can say as a note of elucidation:

Be silent. Let me suppose I am alone,
No light in my eyes, no voice in my ears, with night
That draws down, draws down closer, closer comes.

Times And Locations

Small things, like the turning of a key,
open, as light does a knot of petals, the mind locked
lost in a dead routine.

Things small enough to have seeped through the
  pores,
the nerves, the blood, into the brain,
till they are forgotten, if ever remembered, and you,
                                        and me.

You smile. You clutch my hand.
Lovingly and sadly I feel the hard skin of the palm
and its warmth touches me like a whole body.

Such incredible foliage outside the window.
The sun blazing on its myriad greens.
And the woman sitting at the bed beside,
 a stupid lump on her neck, big as a fist,
tensely counting the puffs at her cigarette—
one—two—three
and the white blue smoke fading
                    gently across the glass partition.

Teatime. We go outside into the sunlight
and wait. We remark the lawn's green,
the empty pond and the heat
falling in thick waves from the brilliant sky.

A steeple clock chimed.
Its leisured sounds lifted ponderously
like great birds:
But we were too frightened to laugh.

Gerard Smyth

Portobello Bridge was conceived during a moment of absolute panaesthesia. Moments when a sensuous awareness of the physical and abstract things described in the poem developed into a state of mesmerisation. This mesmeric effect culminating in the semi-conscious world between dream and reality. The nuance of this 'daydream' world created the poetic tension that afflated the poem.

This experience was, essentially, a visual one. Thus, the need to devise the poem in a visual form—hopefully, this was achieved by constructing the poem in a series of images, with emphasis on detail: an evocation of the scene as it was observed. And it was this sensitive observation that is the centre and the ambience of the poem.

Portobello Bridge

Cool trees send leaves along canal banks
and the water shivers like sensations.

All sounds suffocate in the cotton-silence
that occurs,
           soundless as snow,
in the arc of darkness beneath the bridge.

Pram in the water, filmed in angry rust:
a recent nightmare in the world
                of pinkeen sleep.

Nothing special in the reeds:
                they rattle a laugh
as if tickled by the hurrying breeze
that halts a ghastly kite of flies
                and slows the fog
                of a dog's curling breath.

I think small graves are smothered up
in places of violent growth.

                The water vertigoes
                into a bullseye of circles,
                vexed by darts of rain,
or else,
                the stones from children's games.

The only passer is an old man
who remembers the brightness of a clinic
and the nurse's chill hands.

This daydream is a strange device
of the senses and the elements,
here on Portobello Bridge.

Eugene Watters

*Lavinia Sheridan, a Doctor of Heidelberg, settled in
Ballinasloe, and spent over 50 years as organist in St.
Michael's. As Director of the Choral Society, she produced
Handel, Verdi, Mozart . . . in our limestone Town Hall. High
up in the loft of the neo-Gothic spire (Pugin) she played
Beethoven, Chopin, Sibelius, (me word) Mendelssohn to the
crowds swarming out from last Mass . . .*

*Coming back from her funeral (last January) in our field of
limestone crosses, I tried to express the terrible sense of
something dead and done-for that was shaking my personal
bones; in a simple form that a few at least of the local people
might read. The dull para-rime down through beats in my mind
like a muffled funeral bell. For Lavinia, and for far more—for
the structure, the Church and the whole 2000 years of history
that in our time has whimpered out.*

The Dead Music
For Lavinia Sheridan

Back from the City of Stones, crossing the river
into Main Street, mist and gasoline,
dumb Sunday windows setting the winterscene:
We enter again into the confusion of living.

Grey town, grey sky,
the Lazy Wall, the antique Market Square,
and the remote beauty of a Gothic Spire
in the long melancholy of a mouldering air.

One wanders in, as to a tomb,
no flowers, no ghosts, a well-swept sepulchre,
no Michael now twirling his skirts like a dancer
above the coils of the Confusion.

Lady, here your past is petrified. A shell,
silent, the stone vibrates to the memory
as if one fingering it might feel
the long procession of the harmonies

spirit to spirit relaying the requiems,
the ideal passions and the bethlehems
of Rome, Athens, Vienna, Heidelberg
to our town in the turfbogs

till aging fingers aged.
Now the mind, the music and the discipline
have petered out like a Sunday evening
under the miserable mystery of the rain—

Out. Out. Where human lamps are lighting
in little windows watching the night
one sets the word in earth as epitaph
to the Artist, with love.

Richard Weber

This poem was written on my return to Wicklow after three years of living and teaching in the U.S.A. The political situation in America was to some extent responsible for my decision to go home; the invasion of Cambodia and the Kent State killings confirmed my decision. I was not unaware of Ireland's political situation, but it then seemed preferable to witness one's own national problem. The poem was written in a brief lull in Ireland's strife, and when I refer to history in the poem it is more American than Irish history I have in mind. Also in mind was something Geoffrey Grigson had stated in a review in 1970, to the effect that art could have value sometimes insofar as it was not involved with the political situation of the period. In a time of war there could be some value, humanly speaking, in saying that one lives as one can; that while one is aware to the marrow of one's being of others' agony, there is sometimes little use in noting this in the public form of a poem. That surely goes without saying. Nevertheless, I doubt if I could write such a poem now, as after Derry and Aldershot and in the face of whatever horror is to come, all poetry seems marginal.

As to the poem as artefact, I believe and hope there is little obscurity here. The one foreign phrase, mais oui, *is, of course, humorous in intent. The cat was Persian and probably knew that the lingua franca in a bookish household should be French. It amuses me to play with animal sounds, and in another poem—Stephen's Green Revisited—I have some ducks saying, Not 'quack, quack', but 'aqua, aqua'.*

With regard to the shape of the poem, long before Lowell and Berryman played around with the sonnet form I was writing fourteen-line poems that were not sonnets. Winter in Ballyknockan should have been such another, but my thoughts ran on. In poems of this kind I usually aim for five stresses to the line, and the line is often iambic. The inner ear is always the arbiter, and it will be found that not all the lines have five stresses.

Winter in Ballyknockan

The house heaving, rocking to claps of wind,
The fire grumbling low in its red throat,
Our daughter talking, crying in her sleep,
The cat, owl-eyed, *mais-oui*-ing to be let in,
The coffee bubbling to subdued electric power.
More books on the table than an hour ago,
More lines to write, more food to make and store.
Not much more purpose to this domestic life
Than just to keep alive with wife and child
And cat and food and books and music.
So the life is made, the fire lit and relit
Which must die by dawn as all fires die
That burn towards the final mourning ash.
Keep history out of here a little while.
This night be happy while and though it burns.

Macdara Woods

This poem was written shortly after I had spent some time in hospital. I had recovered; and the year was drawing to an end. A new building had been put up at the end of the garden which reminded me of the architecture of North Africa; it is incongruous to see a style of building designed to give protection from intense sunlight being reproduced at the beginning of an Irish winter. The poem is made up of opposites: the political glass is a mirror, and what you actually see is a reflection. Time and the clock reflect each other. The reference to the fair day is an echo of the line in Macbeth—so fair and foul a day I have not seen. Again the paradox of mirrors; and in this case it further reminds me of the fair days in my childhood in County Meath and the buying and selling of cattle. Childhood and the death of the year reflect each other; March is the month that killed the old cow; my own birthday coincides with the early growth of the beginning of April. The final paradox is that winter is both an end and a beginning.

Late October and I'm out
on a fair day you might say for Dublin
but a cold day for the brieze-block Quasbah
down at the bottom of the garden. Its
lizard eyes thin slits of light
for the sun to hide in corners.
Kennedy's snug is shaped like a ship
time and clock collide
forever taking each other to task
and smoke, like a sluggish anaconda,
recoils and glides on polished glass.
A fair day you might say, for a market,
or driving heavy beasts to the buyers
along the first rime frost of the roadside.
So much for reality: the warm smell of cattle
thick coats, hot whiskies, and ashsticks
prodding the side-stepping bullocks.
So much for late October and the season,
a cruel five month journey into March
and the frozen fields all scorched of shelter
as the clock and the year run down.
La Grande Armée crosses the stubble land
as the teeth of the harrow-rake,
black horses cross the window panes,
glacial patterns, Cossacks in the shape
of scald crows scrabble on the make.
Pinioned in winter the question becomes
year's beginning or season's end.

Appendix

Desmond Egan

Berryman's suicide in January 1972 was in itself one of the saddest events of our saddish times. It can also be seen as a terrifying statement by a great poet on the kind of world he is handing over—over, that is, to you and to me.

It was in Navan hospital that I heard the news of his death.

I hope my mirror does not distort too much (they aren't putting the same stuff into them nowadays) and that, in spite of almost everything, it manages to catch a little light.

For John Berryman

(Because I love so much I lose so much—Tao*)

Riveted girder, blur of carfaces—
the bleary, amused eyes eye
their last.
    No embrace. No hold
: he straightens to be shoved
     out
bridge-steel still
cold in his hurtling fingers

*Version: M. Hartnett, New Writers' Press.

— so simple after all
this final wounding openness
this brief suspension
while he brings throbbing like a stripped nerve
all his kingdom buckling together down
smaller and falling smaller
all his americas
into the river-tarmac
(are there tears in his eyes?
Are there tears in my eyes?)
one last breath
pluming—like Gabriel's message—out of his lips.

To flower
        to ripple away
chopping into the thought-knurls
slowly sinking, sinking deeper
ha ha alas. So long, Berryman.
Christ—who knew the fall, the jerk—
all us save. Enough.

What to do now, this whiskey-bitterness
downed in one smarting gulp, but
burrow into the hospital paper; telly?
— not to think of a kingdom
dangling like a bottle in the empty waters;
and eyes, the unclosed, staring upwards
towards the lighted, the innocent skies.

Michael Hartnett

This is one of the few of my poems that I can say in full. It is a love-poem and was written in 1966. I like it for reasons both sentimental and professional. The hands are my wife's hands: the poem is their equivalent in words. I avoided the use of obvious rhyme such as wan/swan and used less expected words to finalize the stanzas, but the more usual rhymes can be inferred. It is not necessarily my best poem.

Hands

Some white academy of grace
Taught her to dance in perfect ways:
Neck, as locked lily, is not wan
On this great, undulating bird.

Are they indeed your soul, those hands,
As frantic as lace in a wind,
Forever unable to fly
From the beauty of your body?

And if they dance, your five white fawns,
Walking lawns of your spoken word,
What may I do but let linger
My eyes on each luminous bone?

Your hands are music, and phrases
Escape your fingers as they move,
And make the unmappable lands
Quiet orchestra of your limbs.

For I have seen your hands in fields
And called them fluted flowers
Such as the lily is, before
It unleashes its starwhite life:
I have seen your fingernail
Cut the sky
And called it the new moon.

Contributors

BARDWELL, Leland. Living in Dublin; *The Mad Cyclist* ('70); novel pub. 1977.

BECKETT, Samuel. Lives in Paris; best known, of course, for his plays and novels, but has also written some very interesting verse; *Poems in English* ('61); *Complete Poems* ('78); winner of Nobel Prize 1969.

BOLAND Eavan. Writer and critic; living in Dublin; *New Territory* ('67); *The War Horse* ('75).

BOYLAN, Francis. Lives in Madrid; ed. *Ishmael* review.

CASEY, Juanita. Has now settled in Sneem, Kerry; published two novels; *Horse by the River* ('69).

Ní CHUILLEANÁIN, Eiléan. Eng. lecturer, T.C.D.; *Acts and Monuments* ('72); *Odysseus Meets the Ghosts of the Women* ('73); *Sites of Ambush* ('75); *Cork* ('77) *The Second Voyage* ('78).

CLARKE, Austin. Pub. include: *Collected Poems* ('36); *Later Poems* ('61); *Flight to Africa* ('63); *Old Fashioned Pilgrimage* ('67); *The Echo at Coole* ('68); also novels and verse dramas; *Collected Poems* ('75). Mr. Clarke died in '74.

COFFEY, Brian. Now teaching in London; publications include: *Third Person* ('38); *Monster* ('66); *The Time The Place* ('69); *Selected Poems* ('71); *The Big Laugh* ('76).

CRONIN, Anthony. Writer, broadcaster, novelist, critic, now living near Ringsend; *Longer Contemporary Poems* ('66); (with others); *Poems* ('67); *Collected Poems* ('73).

DEANE, Seamus. Lives near Killiney; Assoc. Prof. of English, U.C.D.; *Gradual Wars* ('72); *Rumours* ('77).

DURCAN, Paul. Living in Cork; *Poetry Now* (with 3 others) ('75); *O Westport in the Light of Asia Minor* ('75); *Teresa's Bar* ('76).

EGAN, Desmond. From Athlone; now teaches in Newbridge; publications include: *Midland* ('73); *Leaves* ('75); *Siege!* ('77); *Woodcutter* ('78); *Athlone?* ('79).

FALLER, Kevin. Living in Clontarf; editor in Dublin newspaper; dramatist as well as poet; *Island Lyrics* ('63); *Lament for the Bull Island* ('73).

FALLON, Padraic. An Athenry man; wrote several verse plays for radio as well as for theatre; *Collected Poems* ('74). Mr. Fallon died in '74.

FARREN, Robert. Now retired from R.T.E. Radio; as well as plays, pub. include *Selected Poems* (1951).

FIACC, Padraic. Returned from U.S. to Glengormley, Antrim; *By the Black Stream* ('69); *Odour of Blood* ('73); Edited *The Wearing of the Black* ('74); *Nights in the Bad Place* ('77).

GIBBON, Monk. Living in Sandymount; pub. include: *The Tremulous String* ('26); *This Insubstantial Pageant* ('51); *The Velvet Bow* ('72).

HARTNETT, Michael. Lives and works in Co. Limerick; *Anatomy of a Cliché* ('68); *Selected Poems* ('70); *Tao* ('71); *Gipsy Ballads* ('73); *A Farewell to English* ('75); *The Retreat of Ita Cagney* ('75); *Poems* ('77); *Prisoners* ('77).

HEANEY, Seamus. Lecturer in Carysfort Training College; left Belfast and now lives in Dublin; *Death of a Naturalist* ('66); *A Door into the Dark* ('69); *Wintering Out* ('72); *North* ('75).

HEWITT, John. Has retired home to Ulster from directorship of Coventry art gallery; *No Rebel Ward* ('48); *Collected Poems* ('68); *The Rhyming Weavers* ('74); *Out of My Time* ('74); *Time Enough* ('76); *The Rain Dance* ('78).

HUTCHINSON, Pearse. Has done some translations from Spanish; *Tongue without Hands* ('63); *Expansions* ('69); *Watching the Morning Grow* ('75); *The Frost Is All Over* ('75). Lives in Dublin.

IREMONGER, Valentin. Irish Ambassador; *Reservations* ('45); *Horan's Field and Other Reservations* ('72); also some nice translations from Irish.

JORDAN, John. Critic, living in Dublin; *Patrician Stations* ('72); *A Raft from Flotsam* ('75); *Blood and Stations* ('76).

JOYCE, Trevor. Dubliner; *Pentahedron* ('72); *The Poems of Sweeney Peregrine* ('77).

KELL, Richard. Lecturing in Newcastle Polytechnic; *Control Tower* ('62); *Poems* ('72).

KENNELLY, Brendan. Assoc. Prof. of English, T.C.D.; pub. include: *Selected Poems* ('69); *Love Cry* ('72); *Salvation the Stranger* ('72); *The Voices* ('73); *New and Selected Poems* ('76); *Islandman* ('77); *A Drinking Cup* ('78).

KINSELLA, THOMAS. Prof. of English, Temple University, Philadelphia; prin. publications: *Another September* ('58); *Downstream* ('62); *Nightwalker* ('68); *The Táin* ('69); *Notes from the Land of the Dead* ('72); *Selected Poems* ('73); *New*

Poems ('73); *One* ('74); *A Technical Supplement* ('76); *Song of the Night* ('78); *The Messenger* ('78).

LIDDY, James. Now lives in Wexford; *Esau, My Kingdom for a Drink* ('62); *In a Blue Smoke* ('64); *Blue Mountain* ('68); *Baudelaire's Barroom Flowers* ('76); *Corca Bascinn* ('77).

LONGLEY, Michael. Works with Arts Council, Belfast; *No Continuing City* ('69); *Lares* ('72); *An Exploded View* ('74); *Man Lying on a Wall* ('76).

LUCY, Sean, Prof. of English, U.C.C.; *Five Irish Poets* ('70) (with others).

LYNCH, Brian. Dubliner and art critic; *Endsville* ('67); *No Die Cast* ('69); *Outside the Pheasantry* ('76).

McAULEY, James. Lecturer in English in Washington; *Observations* ('60); *A New Address* ('65); *After the Blizzard* ('75).

McFADDEN, Roy. Solicitor in Belfast; pub. include: *Swords and Ploughshares* ('43); *The Heart's Townland* ('47); *Elegy . . .* ('53); *The Garryowen* ('72); *Versifications* ('77).

McKENNA, James. Sculptor and playwright; living in Chapelizod; *Poems* ('73); play *The Scatterin'* ('77).

McLAUGHLIN, Tom. From Belfast; pub. include *Thus Far, No Surprises* ('71).

MAHON, Derek. Belfastman, now teaching in Coleraine; *Night-Crossing* ('68); *Beyond Howth Head* ('70); *Lives* ('72); *The Snow Party* ('75).

MONTAGUE, John. Lecturer U.C.C.; pub. include: *A Chosen Light* ('67); *Tides* ('70); *The Rough Field* ('72); *A Slow Dance* ('75); *The Great Cloak* ('78).

MOONEY, Brian. Lives in the Burren, Co. Clare; *Island Awakening* ('71).

MULDOON, Paul. Works with BBC in Belfast; *Knowing My Place* ('71); *Poetry Introduction 2* ('72) (with others); *New Weather* ('73); *Mules* ('77).

MURPHY, Donal. Civil Engineer, living near Raheny; included among *Five Irish Poets* ('70).

MURPHY, Hayden. Now lives in England; editor of *Broadsheet.*

MURPHY, Richard. Lives in Cleggan; *The Last Galway Hooker* ('61); *Sailing to an Island* ('63); *The Battle of Aughrim* ('68); *High Island* ('74).

MURRAY, Paul. Belfast priest; *Ritual Poems* ('71).

O'GRADY, Desmond. Lives in Greece; *The Dark Edge of Europe* ('67); *The Dying Gaul* ('68); *Hellas* ('71); *Separations* ('73); *The Gododdin* ('77); *Sing Me Creation* ('77); *A Limerick Rake* ('78).

ORMSBY, Frank. Teacher in Belfast; *Ripe for Company* ('72); *Business As Usual* ('73); *A Store of Candles* ('77).

PAYNE, Basil. Critic, translator; *Sunlight on a Square* ('61); *Love in the Afternoon* ('71); *Another Kind of Optimism* ('74).

RYAN, Richard. Now working in Irish Embassy; *Ledges* ('70); *Poetry Introduction 2* ('72) (with others); *Ravenswood* ('73).

SIMMONS, James. Eng. lecturer University of Coleraine; publications include: *Energy to Burn* ('71); *The Long Summer Still to Come* ('74); *West Strand Visions* ('76); *Judy Garland and the Cold War* ('77); *Selected Poems* ('78).

SMITH, Michael. Teaches in Dublin; pub. include *Dedications* ('68); *Times and Locations* ('72); translations of Machado, *Soledades* (74); *Pilgrimage* ('76).

SMYTH, Gerard. Works in Dublin paper; *The Flags are Quiet* ('69); *Twenty Poems* ('70), *Orchestra of Silence* ('71); *World Without End* ('77).

WATTERS, Eugene. From Ballinasloe, but lives near Carlow; playwright, novelist and critic; best known in Irish; pub. in English include: *The Weekend of Dermot and Grace* ('64); *New Passages* ('73).

WEBER, Richard. Now living in Wicklow; *Lady and Gentleman* ('63); *Stephen's Green Revisited* ('68); *A Few Small Ones* ('71)

WOODS, Macdara. Living in Dublin; pub. include *Decimal D. Sec.* ('70); *Early Morning Matins* ('73).

Acknowledgements

To Calder and Boyars and Samuel Beckett for Beckett's Poem from *Poems in English;* to Chatto and Windus for *Arches* from *Differences* by Richard Kell; to The Dolmen Press for: *The Straying Student* from *Later Poems* by Austin Clarke, *Weir Bridge* from the *Collected Poems* of Padraic Fallon, *Ballydavid Pier* from *Nightwalker* by Thomas Kinsella, *Hands* from *Anatomy of a Cliché* by Michael Hartnett, *The Master Plan* from *Horan's Field and Other Reservations* by Valentin Iremonger, *Times and Locations* from *Times and Locations* by Michael Smith; to Faber and Faber for *The Field Hospital* from *New Weather* by Paul Muldoon and for *Servant Boy* from *Wintering Out* by Seamus Heaney; to Gill and Macmillan for poems by Basil Payne and Michael Longley; to The Irish University Press for *Roots* from *Gradual Wars* by Seamus Deane; to The Mercier Press for poems by Sean Lucy and by Donal Murphy from *Five Irish Poets;* to Gallery Press for *Deaths and Engines* by *Eiléan Ní Chuilleanáin,* and for *Something is Missing* by Brendan Kennelly; to The Goldsmith Press Ltd. for *For John Berryman* from *Midland* by Desmond Egan, for *Summer '69* from *Poems* by James McKenna, for *Blackbird* from *Lament for Bull Island* by Kevin Faller, for *A Christian Soldier Song* from *Odour of Blood* by Padraic Fiacc; to The New Writers' Press for poems by: Leland Bardwell, Anthony Cronin, Trevor Joyce, Paul Murray and Gerard Smyth; to the New York Review of Books for *The Reading Lesson* © 1972 by Richard Murphy; to The Oxford University Press for *Edvard Munch* from *Lives* by Derek Mahon; to A.D. Peters and Co. & MacGibbon and Kee for *All Legendary Obstacles* from *A Chosen Light* by John Montague; to Ulsterman Publications for poems by Tom McLaughlin and Frank Ormsby.
We wish also to acknowledge Ms. Ewa Gargulinska who designed the cover of this second edition.